Who Are You?

Chinese Zodiac

Virginia Loh-Hagan

Published in the United States of America by Cherry Lake Publishing Group
Ann Arbor, Michigan
www.cherrylakepublishing.com

Reading Adviser: Marla Conn, MS, Ed., Literacy specialist, Read-Ability, Inc.
Book Designer: Felicia Macheske

Photo Credits: © SewCream/Shutterstock.com, cover; © vixenkristy/Shutterstock.com, cover; © Vadym Stock/Shutterstock.com, 5; © NASA images/Shutterstock.com, 6; © Rocketclips, Inc./Shutterstock.com, 9; © Anthony Feoutis/Shutterstock.com, 11; © AhXiong/Shutterstock.com, 12; © cynoclub/Shutterstock.com, 15; © Chris Singshinsuk/Shutterstock.com, 17; © Interpass/Shutterstock.com, 18; © Prostock-studio/Shutterstock.com, 20; © Romolo Tavani/Shutterstock.com, 22; © Frederic Legrand - COMEO/Shutterstock.com, 25; © Monkey Business Images/Shutterstock.com, 27; © Chaiwat Hemakom/Shutterstock.com, 29

Graphics Throughout: © AKaiser/Shutterstock.com; © galastudio/Shutterstock.com; © tanyabosyk/Shutterstock.com; © ViSnezh/Shutterstock.com; © MARINA ARABADZHI/Shutterstock.com; © Alisa Burkovska/Shutterstock.com

Copyright © 2021 by Cherry Lake Publishing Group

All rights reserved. No part of this book may be reproduced or utilized in any form or by any means without written permission from the publisher.

45th Parallel Press is an imprint of Cherry Lake Publishing Group.

Library of Congress Cataloging-in-Publication Data

Names: Loh-Hagan, Virginia, author.
Title: Chinese zodiac / by Virginia Loh-Hagan.
Description: Ann Arbor , Michigan : Cherry Lake Publishing, 2020.
| Series: Who are you? | Includes index.
Identifiers: LCCN 2020006986 (print) | LCCN 2020006987 (ebook)
| ISBN 9781534169166 (hardcover) | ISBN 9781534170841 (paperback)
| ISBN 9781534172685 (pdf) | ISBN 9781534174528 (ebook)
Subjects: LCSH: Astrology, Chinese—Juvenile literature. | Zodiac—Juvenile literature.
Classification: LCC BF1714.C5 L73 2020 (print) | LCC BF1714.C5 (ebook) | DDC 133.5—dc23
LC record available at https://lccn.loc.gov/2020006986
LC ebook record available at https://lccn.loc.gov/2020006987

Cherry Lake Publishing Group would like to acknowledge the work of the Partnership for 21st Century Learning, a Network of Battelle for Kids. Please visit *http://www.battelleforkids.org/networks/p21* for more information.

Printed in the United States of America
Corporate Graphics

Dr. Virginia Loh-Hagan is an author, university professor, and former classroom teacher. She is a Yang Fire Dragon. She lives in San Diego, California, with her very tall husband and very naughty dogs. To learn more about her, visit www.virginialoh.com.

Chapter One
Lucky Signs
4

Chapter Two
The Great Race
10

Chapter Three
Beastly Types
16

Chapter Four
Famous Examples
24

Who Are You?
Take the Quiz!
30

Glossary 32

Index 32

Chapter One

Lucky Signs

What is the Chinese zodiac? How is the Chinese zodiac organized? What are the Four Pillars of Destiny?

Have you ever eaten at a Chinese restaurant? There was most likely a placemat in front of you. The placemat had a picture of the Chinese **zodiac**.

The zodiac is an area of the sky. The sun, moon, stars, and planets move in this area. The area is divided into 12 parts. Each part is connected with a time of year. Each part has a name and a **symbol**. Symbols are things or signs. They stand for an idea.

Some people believe these symbols affect humans. These symbols control people's personalities. People also believe these symbols control relationships and **destinies**. Destinies are people's futures.

The zodiac is tied to the sun and the movement of Earth.

The Chinese zodiac is a cycle of 12 years. This cycle repeats itself. Each year is represented by an animal. Each animal has special traits and lucky meanings. People born in a certain year have that animal's traits.

The Chinese zodiac starts on the first day of Chinese New Year. This is the first day of the **lunar** year. Lunar means having to do with the moon. Chinese New Year is in January or February.

The Chinese zodiac follows Jupiter's **orbit**. Orbits are paths that planets follow. Jupiter takes 12 years to orbit the sun. This is called the "great year". The cycle repeats every 5 great years. Every 60th year is a golden year.

> Your animal year comes around every 12 years.
> This happens when you're 12, 24, 36, 48, 60, 72, 84, or 96.
> When is your next animal year?

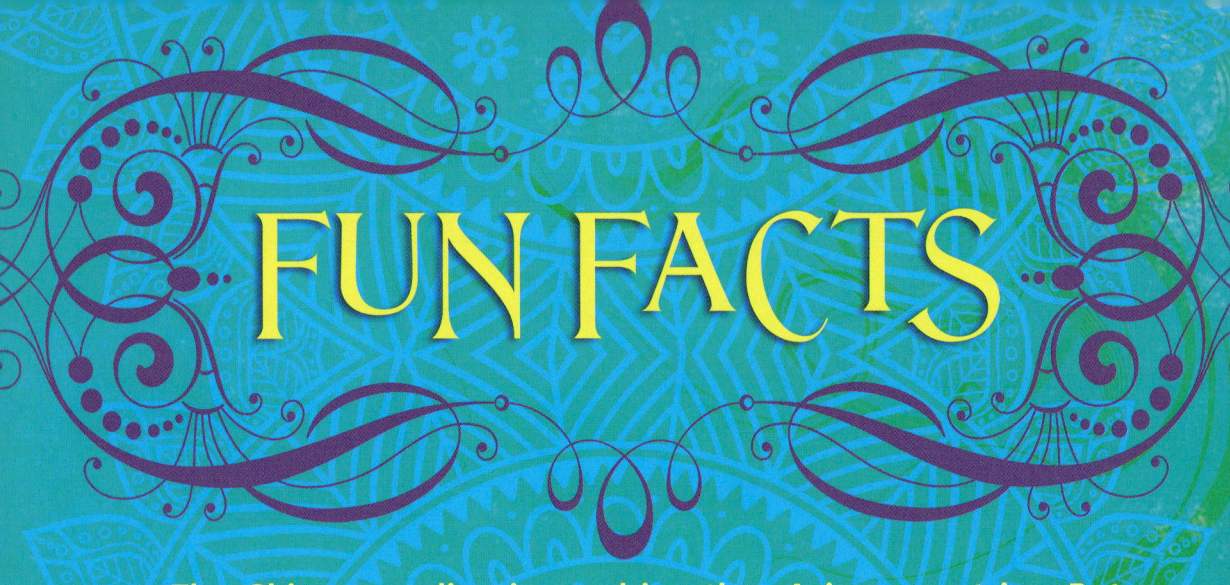

FUN FACTS

* The Chinese zodiac is used in other Asian countries. But some animals are different. For example, Vietnamese people use Buffalo instead of Ox. They use Cat instead of Rabbit.

* Some Chinese people use the zodiac to get married. They hire astrologers to make good matches. They only marry people with the right signs.

* Some Chinese people plan to have babies around the Chinese zodiac. For example, there were lots of babies born in 2000 and 2012. These are Dragon years. People wanted their babies to be Dragons.

* In ancient times, people didn't have clocks. Ancient means a time long ago. They used the 12 zodiac animals to tell the time. Each zodiac sign represented 2 hours. For example, Dog hours were 7 to 9 p.m.

The Four **Pillars** of Destiny guide a person's path through life. Pillars are strong supports. They hold things up. The Four Pillars are birth years, months, days, and hours. Year pillars are connected to birth-year animals. They represent basic personalities. Month pillars represent deeper selves. Animal signs connected to months are called "inner animals." Day pillars represent everyday personalities. Animal signs connected to days are called "true animals." Hour pillars represent personalities that come out when relaxed or under stress. Animal signs connected to hours are called "secret animals."

Your birth month represents information about your family or childhood. It's the most important in determining your fate. What is your birth month?

Chapter Two

THE GREAT RACE

How did the Chinese zodiac develop? What did ancient Chinese astronomers and astrologers do? What is the myth behind the Chinese zodiac?

Astronomy is a science. It's the study of outer space. **Astrology** is a practice. It looks at how space objects affect human lives. Chinese people closely link astronomy and astrology. The Chinese zodiac goes back to the Zhou **dynasty** (1046–256 BCE). Dynasty means a ruling family. The Chinese zodiac became popular during the Han dynasty. This time period was around the 2nd century BCE to 2nd century CE.

During the Han dynasty, Chinese people developed the idea of harmony between heaven, earth, and water. They developed the concepts of **yin** and **yang**. Yin is dark energy. Yang is light energy. The universe has both energies. Both energies fight against each other. They also work together.

Practice self-care so you have balance between yin and yang. Do you feel stressed? Or do you feel relaxed?

In ancient China, emperors hired astronomers. These astronomers' main job was to chart time. They announced the first day of the month. They predicted **lunar eclipses**. Lunar eclipses are when the moon passes into Earth's shadow. Ancient astronomers watched the skies. They made records. They studied space objects. They tracked Jupiter's orbit. They watched it move around the sun. This formed the basic ideas of the Chinese zodiac.

Emperors also hired astrologers. Ancient astrologers interpreted what the astronomers found. They told fortunes. They made predictions. They helped emperors make decisions.

Hire a Chinese astrologer. Get your charts read. Does knowing your future scare you or excite you?

EXPLAINED BY SCIENCE

The Chinese zodiac follows the lunar calendar. The lunar calendar is based on the monthly cycles of the moon's phases. The moon orbits around Earth. The half of the moon that faces the sun will be lit up. The different shapes of the lit part that can be seen from Earth are known as moon phases. Each phase repeats itself every 29.5 days. The moon goes through 8 major phases. A "new moon" is when the moon cannot be seen. It occurs when the moon is directly between Earth and the sun. A "full moon" is when we can see the entire moon. This happens when the moon is on the opposite side of Earth from the sun. In the other phases, the moon waxes and wanes. Wax means to increase. Wane means to decrease. The moon looks like a crescent. It looks like a half moon. The time it takes for the moon to go from one "new moon" to the next is called a synodic month. This is also called a lunation.

Chinese people also created **myths**. Myths are stories. They explain things. They help people make sense of the world.

In a popular myth, the Jade Emperor hosts a "great race." He calls all the animals to cross a river. But only 12 animals can win. Cat and Rat can't swim. So they hop on Ox's back. Rat pushes Cat into the water. Rat jumps ahead of Ox and runs to the emperor. This is why Rat is the first animal. Pig is the last one because he always stopped to eat. Cat never makes it because he drowns. This myth explains the order of the zodiac animals. The years are named for each animal in the order they reach the emperor. It also explains why Cat isn't in the Chinese zodiac.

Read different versions of this myth. Which one is your favorite version?

Chapter Three

Beastly Types

What are the 12 Chinese zodiac animals? Why is the Dragon special? What are the 4 trines? What are the 5 elements?

The Chinese zodiac has 12 animal signs. The order of the animals is Rat, Ox, Tiger, Rabbit, Dragon, Snake, Horse, Goat (or Ram), Monkey, Rooster (or Chicken), Dog, and Pig.

The Dragon is the only mythical animal in the zodiac. It's not a real animal. But it's the luckiest animal. Dragons are important in Chinese culture. They're good luck symbols. They're power symbols. People born in the year of the Dragon are thought to be extra lucky.

There are 4 **trines**. Trines are groups of 3. Each trine has 3 animals. They share personality traits. Some traits are **positive**. Positive means strengths. Some traits are **negative**. Negative means weaknesses.

Learn more about your specific animal sign.
Do a google search. What does it say about you?

The first trine includes the Rat, Dragon, and Monkey. These signs are powerful. They're smart. They're charming. They have a lot of energy. They attract people. They make great leaders. They're winners. They can do really good things. But they can be unpredictable. They can be jealous. They can be tricky. They can be selfish.

The second trine includes the Ox, Snake, and Rooster. These signs are hard workers. They're great planners. They're fair leaders. They're smart. They're patient. They're loyal. They follow rules. They don't give up. But they can be stubborn. They can be **vain**. Vain people think too highly of their looks and abilities. They can be judgmental.

Make a list of traits. Compare your traits to the Chinese zodiac descriptions. How true are they?

The third trine includes the Tiger, Horse, and Dog. These signs are kind and loving. They have big dreams. They're independent. They get excited. They have honor. They speak very well. But they can be impulsive. They can break rules. They can be moody. They can hold grudges.

The fourth trine includes the Rabbit, Goat, and Pig. These signs tend to be artists. They're creative. They seek beauty. They're calm. They have good manners. They're shy. They're the best friends to have. But they can be too trusting. They can also be negative. They may have a hard time making decisions. They may question themselves.

> **Figure out your friends' zodiac signs. Are they in your trine? Do you get along?**

REAL-LIFE CONNECTION

Most Chinese people think people born in a Goat or Ram year are unlucky. Goats are thought to become followers rather than leaders. A Chinese aunt told her niece, "Giving birth to a Goat baby is definitely a bad idea." Some Chinese people believe Goat babies cause bad things to happen. For example, they think Goats' parents will die. They think Goats will have unhappy marriages. They think Goats will never have children. Northern Chinese people tend to believe this more. They believe that only 1 in 10 Goats are lucky. Young Chinese people won't date Goats. There are support groups for Goats. They're victims of "zodiac-shaming." This is when people are treated unfairly because of their zodiac signs. Officials don't want these beliefs to affect birth rates. They don't want people to avoid having babies in Goat years. They think this is an "unfair and outdated superstition." Superstitions are beliefs that aren't based on facts or reason.

Animals in the same trine often make the best of friends. They get along. Their enemies tend to be animals in other trines.

Animals can also be sorted by **elements**. Elements are parts of a whole. The 5 elements are wood, fire, earth, metal, and water. Elements can help each other. For example, water feeds wood. Wood feeds fire. Fire creates earth. Earth makes metals. Metals make water. Or the elements can hurt each other. For example, fire melts metal. Metal chops wood. Wood breaks up earth. Earth takes in water. Water puts out fires.

Wood animals are Tiger and Rabbit. They're kind. Fire animals are Horse and Snake. They're strong and brave. Metal animals are Monkey and Rooster. They're fair. Water animals are Rat and Pig. They're wise. Earth animals are Dragon, Dog, Ox, and Goat. They're honest.

> Figure out your family members' element signs. How do you help each other? How do you hurt each other?

Chapter Four

Famous Examples

Who is Barack Obama? Who is Queen Victoria? Who is Dr. Martin Luther King Jr.?

Barack Hussein Obama is a famous Ox. Obama was the 44th U.S. president. He's the first African American U.S. president. He fights for civil rights. He writes books. He's a great speaker.

He was born on August 4, 1961. A Chinese astrologer studied his sign. It was determined that Obama was born on a water Rooster hour. He was born on an earth Snake day. He was born in a wood Goat month. He was born in a metal Ox year. He matches his Chinese zodiac. He's a hard worker. He's always busy. He has many friends.

The year 2009 was Obama's first year as president. It's also the year he won the Nobel Peace Prize. It was an Ox year.

Look up famous people with your Chinese zodiac sign. Who else is your sign?

Queen Victoria ruled the United Kingdom of Great Britain and Ireland. She ruled from 1837 to 1901. She also ruled over India. Her rule was called the Victorian Era. She expanded British lands. She made many great changes. She led her nation to be a global power.

She was born on May 24, 1819. This means she was a Rabbit. Queen Victoria even compared herself to a rabbit. This was because she had 9 children. Rabbits have big families.

Rabbits are proud. They're quiet but strong. They're also romantic. Rabbits fall deeply in love. This was true of Queen Victoria. She loved Prince Albert. They wrote many love letters. When Albert died, Queen Victoria wore black for over 40 years until she died.

Look up the Chinese zodiac sign of your favorite person. What is it? Does the person fit the description?

SPOTLIGHT BIOGRAPHY

Gan De was an ancient Chinese astronomer and astrologer. He lived in the 4th century BCE. He's one of the first to make a star catalog. This is a record that lists stars. Gan De recorded dates. He recorded coordinates. Coordinates are sets of numbers that show location. Gan De was also the first to make detailed observations of Jupiter. He studied it closely. He wrote down many details. He described Jupiter as "very large and bright." He saw a "small reddish star" next to Jupiter. This was amazing because he saw it with his naked eye. He didn't have telescopes. He also studied Jupiter's movements. He observed how Jupiter returns to the same place every 12 years. He observed how it disappeared every 370 days. He observed it coming back 30 days later. He also studied 4 other planets and their orbits. He wrote several books. He wrote about Jupiter and stars. He wrote about astrology.

Dr. Martin Luther King Jr. was a civil rights leader. He fought for freedom. He fought for justice. He wanted all people to be treated fairly.

He was born on January 15, 1929. This means he was a metal earth Dragon. Metal earth Dragons are powerful. They have strong beliefs. They're smart. They're charming. They're supportive. They seek peace. They face whatever comes their way. They fight for change. King made many great changes to our nation.

King's day animal is a metal Monkey. This means he had big dreams. King is best known for his "I Have a Dream" speech.

Look up the Chinese zodiac signs that are best matched for you. What are they? Who are you most compatible with?

WHO ARE YOU?
TAKE THE QUIZ!

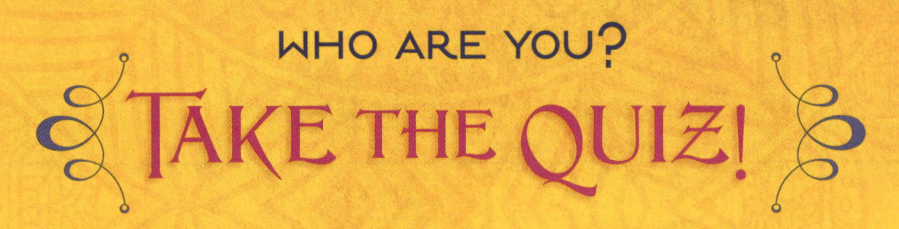

Birth year: What's your basic personality? Your birth year animal gives information about how people view you.

- **1984, 1996, 2008, 2020, 2032, 2044:** You're a Rat. You're witty. You use your resources. You're kind.

- **1985, 1997, 2009, 2021, 2033, 2045:** You're an Ox. You're a hard worker. You're dependable. You're strong.

- **1986, 1998, 2010, 2022, 2034, 2046:** You're a Tiger. You're brave. You're confident. You like competing.

- **1987, 1999, 2011, 2023, 2035, 2047:** You're a Rabbit. You're quiet. You're elegant. You're responsible.

- **1988, 2000, 2012, 2024, 2036, 2048:** You're a Dragon. You're powerful. You're smart. You're enthusiastic.

- **1989, 2001, 2013, 2025, 2037, 2049:** You're a Snake. You're mysterious. You're wise. You're charming.

- **1990, 2002, 2014, 2026, 2038, 2050:** You're a Horse. You have a lot of energy. You're active. You're fair.

- **1991, 2003, 2015, 2027, 2039, 2051:** You're a Goat. You're calm. You're gentle. You think of others' feelings.

- **1992, 2004, 2016, 2028, 2040, 2052:** You're a Monkey. You think quickly. You're curious. You make friends easily.

- **1993, 2005, 2017, 2029, 2041, 2053:** You're a Rooster. You notice everything. You're bold. You make decisions.

- **1994, 2006, 2018, 2030, 2042, 2054:** You're a Dog. You're loyal. You're honest. You're thoughtful.

- **1995, 2007, 2019, 2031, 2043, 2055:** You're a Pig. You're caring. You're generous. You take pride in your work.

DISCLAIMER: All the quizzes and questions in this book are designed for entertainment purposes only. They shouldn't be used as advice. They shouldn't be taken seriously. There is no guarantee of accuracy. But they're fun! To download a copy of this quiz, please visit: https://cherrylakepublishing.com/teaching_guides.

What's your Chinese element? If the last number in your birth year is:

- **0:** Yang metal.
- **1:** Yin metal.
- **2:** Yang water.
- **3:** Yin water.
- **4:** Yang wood.
- **5:** Yin wood.
- **6:** Yang fire.
- **7:** Yin fire.
- **8:** Yang earth.
- **9:** Yin earth.

What are your best matches? People with these animal signs will be your best friends.

- **Rat:** Ox, Dragon, Rabbit
- **Ox:** Rat, Monkey, Rooster
- **Tiger:** Dragon, Horse, Pig
- **Rabbit:** Rat, Goat, Monkey, Dog, Pig
- **Dragon:** Rat, Tiger, Snake
- **Snake:** Dragon, Rooster
- **Horse:** Goat, Tiger
- **Goat:** Rabbit, Horse, Pig
- **Monkey:** Ox, Rabbit
- **Rooster:** Ox, Snake
- **Dog:** Rabbit
- **Pig:** Goat, Tiger, Rabbit

Birth month: What's your "inner animal?" Your birth month animal gives information about your deeper self.

- **December 7 to January 5:** Rat
- **January 6 to February 3:** Ox
- **February 4 to March 5:** Tiger
- **March 6 to April 4:** Rabbit
- **April 5 to May 4:** Dragon
- **May 5 to June 5:** Snake
- **June 6 to July 6:** Horse
- **July 7 to August 6:** Goat
- **August 7 to September 7:** Monkey
- **September 8 to October 7:** Rooster
- **October 8 to November 6:** Dog
- **November 7 to December 6:** Pig

Glossary

astrology (uh-STRAH-luh-jee) the practice of how space objects like stars affect the lives of humans

astronomy (uh-STRAH-nuh-mee) the study or science of outer space

destinies (DES-tuh-neez) fates or futures

dynasty (DYE-nuh-stee) a ruling family

elements (El-uh-muhnts) parts of a whole

lunar (LOO-nur) of the moon

lunar eclipses (LOO-nur ih-KLIPS-iz) times when the moon passes into Earth's shadow

myths (MITHS) traditional stories that explain things people don't understand so that they can make sense of the world

negative (NEG-uh-tiv) weakness

orbit (OR-bit) the path of an object in space

pillars (PIL-urz) strong supports or ideas that hold things up

positive (PAH-zih-tiv) strength

symbol (SIM-buhl) a thing or sign that stands for an idea

trines (TRYNZ) groups of three

vain (VAYN) showing the attitude of someone who thinks very highly of his or her looks and abilities

yang (YANG) light energy

yin (YIN) dark energy

zodiac (ZOH-dee-ak) an imaginary band in the heavens centered on the paths of all the space objects and divided into 12 constellations or signs for astrological purposes

Index

animals, 7, 8, 9, 14, 16–23, 29
astrology, 10, 12, 28
astronomy, 10, 12, 28

balance, 11

calendar, lunar, 13
Cat, 14
Chinese New Year, 7

day pillars, 9, 24, 29
destinies, 4
Dog, 16, 20, 23
Dragon, 16, 19, 23, 29

earth, 10, 23, 24, 29
elements, 23
energy, 10

fire, 23
Four Pillars of Destiny, 9

Gan De, 28
Goat (Ram), 16, 20, 21, 23, 24
golden years, 7, 29
great year, 7

Han dynasty, 10
harmony, 10
heaven, 10
Horse, 16, 20, 23
hour pillars, 9, 24

Jupiter, 7, 12, 28

King, Martin Luther Jr, 29

luck, 16, 21
lunar eclipses, 12

metal, 23, 24, 29
Monkey, 16, 19, 23, 29
month pillars, 9, 24
moon, 4, 13
myths, 14

negative traits, 16

Obama, Barack, 24
Ox, 14, 16, 19, 23, 24

personality, 4, 9, 19, 20
 quiz, 30–31
Pig, 14, 16, 20, 23
positive traits, 16

Rabbit, 16, 20, 23, 26
Ram, 21
Rat, 14, 16, 19, 23
Rooster (Chicken), 16, 19, 23, 24

Snake, 16, 19, 23, 24
sun, 4, 5, 7
superstitions, 21

Tiger, 16, 20, 23
traits, 7, 16, 19, 20, 30–31
trines, 16, 19, 20, 23

Victoria (Queen), 26

water, 10, 23, 24
wood, 23, 24

yang, 10, 11
year pillars, 9, 24
years, 7
yin, 10, 11

zodiac
 cycles, 7
 development of, 10–15
 famous examples, 24–29
 fun facts, 8
 quiz, 30–31
 and science, 13
 what it is, 4–8